T0030072

BIG ASA

GIANT SNAIL

Discovering the World's Most Gigantic Animals

by **Jess Keating**

with illustrations by David DeGrand

Alfred A. Knopf
New York

A NOTE FOR READERS: This book is full of giants, but it's not easy to capture their true size without some help. The banana below is six inches long, and we'll tell you each animal's size in number of bananas. In this way, you can figure out the scale of every animal in the book! These measurements are approximate, but very fun.

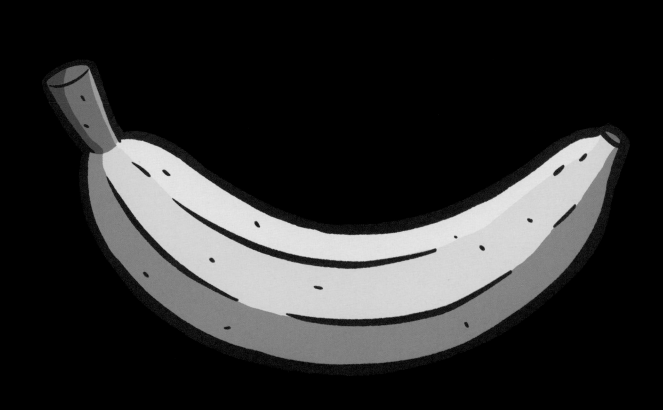

Colossal. Gigantic.
Enormous. BIG!

The biggest animals in the world may look different, but they all have one thing in common: they are immensely WEIRD! We may think that the heaviest, tallest, or hugest animals are all slow, lumbering giants, but there is so much more to these creatures than their awesome size. *BIG* contains multitudes, and it takes all sizes to keep an ecosystem healthy.

Turn the page to see these larger-than-life creatures in a whole new light!

Big as a MALABAR GIANT SQUIRREL

5 bananas (length)

What's the deal with this radiantly robust rodent?! It's a squirrel—but it might not look like one you've seen before! The **MALABAR GIANT SQUIRREL** is a work of art, with beautiful **coloration** from head to toe. But those maroon, cream, red, and yellow patches aren't just for show. Scientists believe their vibrant colors help them **camouflage** with the patches of light and shadow in the forest **canopy.**

Nuts for Trees

In many North American neighborhoods, it's common to see squirrels skittering along the ground, burying their food in the soil. But these colorful giants don't bother with that. In fact, they rarely leave the treetops! Instead of burying their food in the ground, they are almost completely **arboreal,** stashing food stores high in the trees.

Name: Malabar giant squirrel, or Indian giant squirrel

Species name: *Ratufa indica*

Size: The average size of both male and female squirrels is 1 foot 2 inches (36 centimeters) from head to rump, with a tail that is 1 foot 6 inches (46 centimeters) long.

Diet: Flowers, fruit, bark, nuts, bird eggs, and insects

Habitat: These squirrels prefer to live in the upper canopy of trees, residing in **deciduous** and evergreen forests and woodlands of India, in the Western Ghats, Eastern Ghats, and Satpura Range.

Predators and threats: Although they spend most of their time avoiding predators in their high treetop homes, it's thought that snakes, raptors, cats, and **civets** may prey on these animals, as juveniles and adults.

Big as a BLUE WHALE

200 bananas (length)

When it comes to size, no animal on the planet can compete with the **cetaceans.** And in the world of whales, the BLUE WHALE wins by a mile. But that's not all—blue whales are also some of the *loudest* creatures on the planet. They sing **low-frequency** tunes to communicate in the deep, and so far, scientists have divided their songs into nine unique types. Whales from different regions can be identified by their song!

Now, That's a Mouthful!

Get this: the biggest animal in the world survives by eating one of the *smallest!* Each krill is about the size of a paper clip, so blue whales have to eat around 40 million of them every day to fill their bellies. The skin beneath their bottom jaws is equipped with **ventral pleats,** so their throats can expand like balloons. Because of this fab feeding feature, these whales can scoop their own body weight in water!

Name: Blue whale

Species name: *Balaenoptera musculus*

Size: Up to approximately 100 feet (30 meters) long

Diet: While they may accidentally gulp down **amphipods** and **copepods,** blue whales survive by eating krill, krill, and more krill!

Habitat: Blue whales are found in all major ocean basins, with the exception of the Arctic Ocean and Bering Sea. Unlike some other whales, blue whales do not share specific **migration** patterns from year to year and appear to move from area to area for different reasons like mating, feeding, and **calving.**

Predators and threats: These animals were hunted almost to the point of **extinction** by humans, until 1967, when the killing of blue whales was banned. Orcas are one of their only wild predators, choosing younger, smaller whales to hunt.

Big as an AFRICAN GIANT SNAIL

1 banana (length)

The **AFRICAN GIANT SNAIL** is one massively mammoth **mollusk!** These creatures produce an oozy trail of mucus and travel along it using one muscular **foot.** Whenever they find food, they scrape up small bits to eat using a **radula** in their mouths. With thousands of microscopic teeth, this flexible band helps them ingest small morsels. Some species of mollusks have over *100,000* tiny chompers! Luckily, their **voracious** appetites help decompose plant matter and keep the soil tidy.

Don't Try This at Home!

They may be impressively huge, but giant snails are also one of the most **invasive species** on Earth, and this can mean big trouble for humans. Not only do they eat practically any **vegetation** they can find, they've also been known to munch on the stucco walls of people's homes. They can cause so much havoc, it's against the law to own them in the United States!

MUNCH!

Name: Giant African land snail

Species name: *Achatina fulica*

Size: Shells can grow up to 7.9 inches (20 centimeters) long and 2.8 inches (7.1 centimeters) high.

Diet: These snails eat a varied diet of plants, paper, sand, small stones, bones, and even concrete and stucco. Rarely, they may also eat other snails.

Habitat: This species is highly invasive, so despite being native to East Africa, it can be found in many temperate ecosystems, including the tropics, coastlands, forests, scrublands, wetlands, and urban areas around the world, on all continents except Antarctica.

Predators and threats: Many known parasites pose a threat to these snails. Beetles, crabs, birds, and some mammals, like foxes and wild pigs, will all prey on them if given the chance.

Big as a MOOSE

14 bananas (height)

As the largest members of the deer family, moose have a leg up on their smaller cousins. Or rather, several feet up! Some **MOOSE** tower more than ten feet tall, and their massive antlers can be nearly two yards wide. During **rutting season,** moose crash and thrash through the forest, rubbing those antlers against vegetation. Why? The raucous sound sends the message "I'm in charge here!" Large antlers also act as a **parabolic reflector,** helping the moose hear better.

Gettin' Nerdy About Headgear

What's the difference between antlers and horns? Moose and deer have antlers—a single structure made of bone. Horns, which are found on cows, sheep, goats, and antelopes, have two parts: the inner bone and an outer layer of **keratin.** Antlers are shed every year and regrown every spring. But horns stay put, often growing throughout the lifetime of the animal.

THRASH!

Name: Moose

Species name: *Alces alces*

Size: From 4 feet 7 inches to 6 feet 11 inches (1.4–2.1 meters) at the shoulder, with a body length of 7 feet 11 inches to 10 feet 2 inches (2.4–3.1 meters)

Diet: Terrestrial plants, such as flowering plants and willow or birch shoots. In winter, moose may visit roads to lick up the salt scattered to clear snow and ice.

Habitat: Various species of moose can be found throughout Canada, the United States, Europe, and Asia. Moose need well-shaded habitats with lots of edible plants and will travel to protect themselves from extreme heat and cold.

Predators and threats: Wolves, Siberian tigers, mountain lions, and brown bears will all prey on moose if the opportunity arises. Humans hunt them. Moose also can get parasitic brain worms from accidentally eating snails.

Big as a LEATHERBACK SEA TURTLE

11 bananas (length)

A turtle as big as a human?! You betcha! **LEATHERBACK SEA TURTLES** may look bulky on the sand, but their huge, tapered shells are **hydrodynamic,** with long ridges that allow them to cut through the water quickly and gracefully. Unlike other sea turtles, the leatherback's **carapace** isn't hard. Instead, it's flexible and soft!

Startling Spikes!

These aquatic giants sup on seaweed, fish, and other soft creatures, but their favorite food is jellyfish. How do they wrangle and eat slippery, gooey jellyfish tentacles? The secret is in the spikes! Leatherback sea turtles have specialized spikes called **oral papillae** in their mouths and throats. These papillae help the turtles grasp prey and ensure it doesn't escape!

NOM NOM

Name: Leatherback sea turtle

Species name: *Dermochelys coriacea*

Size: Their large, teardrop-shaped bodies can grow from 3 feet 4 inches to 5 feet 8 inches long (1–1.7 meters), weighing up to 1,540 pounds (699 kilograms).

Diet: Jellyfish and other soft-bodied sea life, such as octopuses. They also eat fish and seaweed.

Habitat: These animals are found in tropical and subtropical oceans as far as the Arctic Circle. They return to beaches during nesting seasons.

Predators and threats: Humans are the biggest threat: poachers steal eggs and some kill turtles for meat or hides. Pollution, litter, and fishing gear in the ocean can kill turtles. Hotel lights can also disorient hatchlings trying to find the sea.

Big as a CASSOWARY

11 bananas (height)

In the world of birds, ostriches may hog the spotlight when it comes to size, but it's their cousin the **CASSOWARY** that brings a little flair to the party. Cassowaries are the heaviest birds in Australia, and if you're thinking they look dangerous—you're right! These bulky birds will attack humans if they feel threatened. A five-inch, dagger-like claw on their toe makes for an impressive weapon!

Keep Cool in Style

Wondering what's up with that snazzy, pointy helmet? The structure on top of a cassowary's head is called a **casque.** For centuries, scientists were unsure of its purpose. Was it used in defense? Or to amplify the cassowary's noisy calls? As it turns out, this large horn-like hat could be used as a thermal **radiator,** helping it keep cool in the hot Australian summers.

Name: Southern cassowary

Species name: *Casuarius casuarius*

Size: 4 feet 2 inches to 5 feet 7 inches (127–170 centimeters) from head to tail and 4 feet 9 inches to 5 feet 9 inches (1.5–1.8 meters) tall. They are the second-heaviest bird on Earth, weighing up to 187 pounds (85 kilograms).

Diet: They are known to eat more than two hundred species of fruit, along with fungi, small frogs, birds, fish, mice, and insects.

Habitat: Tropical rainforests, mangrove stands, and savanna forests of northeastern Australia, New Guinea, and Indonesia

Predators and threats: Human activities, like logging, and habitat loss are threats to these birds. Their eggs may be eaten by **feral** animals, and they are sometimes struck by cars along roadways.

Big as a POLAR BEAR

20 bananas (length)

No book of giants would be complete without the biggest bear on Earth! **POLAR BEARS** are the largest land **carnivores** and can weigh as much as *ten* full-grown men. It takes a lot of food to keep a polar bear belly full, so they will swim for days at a time in search of prey. Strong, wide paws make perfect paddles, and black skin under their white fur helps absorb heat from the sun to keep them cozy in chilly Arctic waters.

Saunter to Stay Cool

Have you ever noticed that polar bears always seem to walk at a slow, leisurely pace? They're not lazy—they're just cooling off. While polar bears need to regulate their temperature against the cold, they *also* need to worry about overheating! Their body temperatures can get too high when they run (especially in summer!), so most bears plod along over the landscape as they hunt.

Name: Polar bear

Species name: *Ursus maritimus*

Size: These creatures grow to between 7 feet 10 inches and 9 feet 10 inches in length (2.4–3 meters), with males averaging nearly 1,000 pounds (454 kilograms); females are roughly half the size and weigh between 331 and 551 pounds (150–250 kilograms).

Diet: Polar bears thrive on high-fat diets of seals, particularly ringed and bearded seals. They will also eat a wide variety of foods when available, including dolphins, reindeer, rodents, and plant matter.

Habitat: Regions of the Arctic Circle, including Canada, Alaska, Russia, Denmark, and Norway

Predators and threats: Melting sea ice is a major concern. Polar bears need an ice platform to hunt seals. Without it, they can starve or even drown. They also den underground, and warmer winters can cause their roofs to collapse.

Big as an ATLAS MOTH

2 bananas (wingspan)

Are you ready to meet a real behe-*moth*? With its vibrant, sturdy wings and enormous body, the ATLAS MOTH has a wingspan about as wide as the cover of the book you're reading. Look closely at those wing tips: Do they remind you of anything? Some scientists believe their wing tips evolved to resemble snake heads, scaring off potential predators!

The Downside of Being Big

You might think this giant moth needs to eat a whole lot of food to power those gargantuan wings and stay healthy. But guess what: they *can't* eat as adults! Instead, they must eat as much as possible as caterpillars, and find a mate quickly when they're fully grown moths. It takes a lot of energy to power such a large body, so Atlas moths can only survive for one to two weeks before they starve.

Name: Atlas moth

Species name: *Attacus atlas*

Size: Wingspans measure about 9.4 inches (24 centimeters), with a surface area of 25 inches² (161 centimeters²).

Diet: As larvae, these creatures eat plant matter, including cinnamon, evergreen, citrus, privet, willow, sugar apple, and mango trees. As adults, they do not eat.

Habitat: The tropical forests, lowlands, and shrublands of South Asia, Southeast Asia, and East Asia

Predators and threats: Atlas moths are eaten by most mammals and birds, as well as some ants. Certain species of flies may also attack them and **parasitize** their larvae. Humans have also used their large cocoons as purses.

Big as a CAPYBARA

8 bananas (length)

Ever see a rodent the size of a large dog? Meet the **CAPYBARA!** These mellow, hairy creatures are the world's largest rodents, and they're well equipped for their **semi-aquatic** lifestyle. Their brittle fur dries quickly as they move in and out of the water. You'd think they'd sink in the mud, but webbed feet with hoof-like claws help their bulky bods stay out of the squishy terrain.

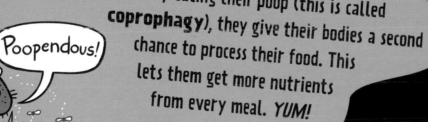

Breakfast of Champions!

You might start the day with a bowl of cereal or some toast, but capybaras have a fantastically funky food source. They eat poop! Specifically, their *own* poop. These animals eat plants and enjoy a diet very high in hard-to-digest grasses. By eating their poop (this is called **coprophagy**), they give their bodies a second chance to process their food. This lets them get more nutrients from every meal. *YUM!*

Poopendous!

Name: Capybara

Species name: *Hydrochoerus hydrochaeris*

Size: Roughly 2 feet tall (61 centimeters) at the shoulder, with a body length between 3 feet 2 inches and 4 feet 2 inches (100–128 centimeters)

Diet: Water plants, grasses, grains, melons, squashes, and reeds. These animals also eat their own poop.

Habitat: Swampy regions of Central and South America, particularly in areas bordering ponds, rivers, streams, and lakes

Predators and threats: Capybaras are threatened by deforestation, poaching, and habitat destruction. They are also hunted by humans for their meat and hides. Today, some humans farm capybaras for their meat.

Big as a HARPY EAGLE

13 bananas (wingspan)

HARPY EAGLES are one of the biggest and *strongest* raptors in the world. Life isn't easy when you live in the jungle with jaguars, monkeys, and snakes, but the harpy eagle has what it takes to thrive. Four-inch claws? Check. Sharp eyesight? Check. Awesome hairdo? Check! Despite being so large, harpy eagles have relatively short wings—this helps them twist and turn in their rainforest environment.

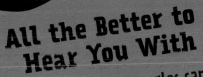

All the Better to Hear You With

As a top predator, harpy eagles can take down all sorts of prey, including porcupines, sloths, and monkeys. But first, they have to listen up and find them! The feathers around their faces form a circle, which helps direct sound to their ears. They can lift and lower this "facial disk" using muscles in their face. By doing so, they can track prey by simply turning their heads and "tuning in." They're known to perch perfectly still for nearly twenty-four hours, waiting for prey!

Name: Harpy eagle

Species name: *Harpia harpyja*

Size: About 2 feet 11 inches to 3 feet 5 inches tall (89–104 centimeters), females being larger than males; wingspans up to 6 feet 6 inches (2 meters)

Diet: Harpy eagles eat mainly arboreal animals, such as monkeys, snakes, iguanas, sloths, coatis, opossums, and birds. They will also munch on porcupines, anteaters, deer, and rodents.

Habitat: Forested areas of southern Mexico to northern Argentina. They tend to nest in silk cotton trees, 90 to 140 feet (27–43 meters) above the ground.

Predators and threats: These animals do not migrate, and they need large expanses of forest to survive. Logging, poaching, and nest destruction can threaten them. Because adult pairs can only raise one eaglet every two years, populations grow slowly.

Big as an ELEPHANT SEAL

40 bananas (length)

Check out that "trunk"! An **ELEPHANT SEAL**'s bulbous nose is nothing to sneeze at, but it's also *inflatable*! By filling this one-and-a-half-foot-long **proboscis** with air, a male elephant seal can make itself look even more menacing. This is important when you're fighting for mating rights to a **harem** of female seals! That extra-large nose also amplifies its grunts, bellows, and groans, so they can be heard from several miles away.

I Mustache You About Those Whiskers!

It isn't easy to find food in the deep, dark waters of the South Atlantic Ocean. Luckily, elephant seals are up to the task. Their eyes are about ten times more sensitive to light than our human ones, allowing them to spot **bioluminescent** prey easily. Their long, bristly whiskers, also known as **vibrissae**, can sense the environment much like your own fingers. This gives them an edge in the hunt for fish and squid.

Name: Southern elephant seal

Species name: *Mirounga leonina*

Size: Males can reach up to 20 feet long (6.1 meters), with females reaching up to 10 feet (3 meters); males may weigh anywhere from 4,900 to 8,800 pounds (2,223–3,992 kilograms), while females are much smaller, weighing 880 to 1,980 pounds (399–898 kilograms).

Diet: Squid and fish, which they hunt at depths of 1,300 to 3,300 feet (396–1,006 meters)

Habitat: The subpolar and polar beaches and surrounding waters of the Southern Hemisphere

Predators and threats: Due to their valuable blubber, these seals were hunted to near extinction in the twentieth century. Today, climate change and overfishing pose problems. Orcas, leopard seals, and sharks will all prey on them.

Big as an OCEAN SUNFISH

22 bananas (length)

Nope, this fish isn't missing a tail—it's a fully formed **OCEAN SUNFISH** in all its glory! Ocean sunfish are one of the biggest bony fishes on the planet, and they're also known as one of the most fertile. Scientists have found that these fish lay more eggs than any other **vertebrate**—up to 300 *million* in a single **spawning season.** Now *that's* an epic family tree!

Soak Up the Sun!

Why are these gentle giants named "sunfish"? Because they love to sunbathe! Ocean sunfish swim in both **epipelagic** and **mesopelagic** zones of the ocean, which means they like the surface *and* deeper waters. The deep ocean is cold, and after a dive, sunfish will often drift back up, letting the sun's rays warm up their bodies. By harnessing the sun's energy, they keep their body temperature stable and healthy.

Name: Ocean sunfish

Species name: *Mola mola*

Size: They average 5 feet 11 inches (1.8 meters) in length and weigh between 545 and 2,205 pounds (247–1,000 kilograms); some of the larger specimens have measured up to 10 feet 10 inches long (3.3 meters), with weights up to 5,100 pounds (2,313 kilograms).

Diet: They are **generalist predators** and will eat a variety of food, including jellyfish, worms, crustaceans, squid, fish larvae, sea squirts, sponges, and sea stars.

Habitat: Sunfish can be found in all tropical and temperate oceans.

Predators and threats: Sea lions, orcas, sharks, bluefin tuna, and mahi-mahi will prey on them. They are considered a **delicacy** to some humans, and parts of their bodies are used in medicine. They can choke on floating litter or get caught in fishing nets.

Big as a GIANT ANTEATER

16 bananas (length)

With its long, tubular snout and bushy swoosh of a tail, it's hard to tell if this animal is coming or going! True to its name, the **GIANT ANTEATER** is built for finding—and *eating*—ants. Its sense of smell is thought to be *forty times* stronger than that of a human, which enables it to sniff out tasty anthills and termite mounds. Once it finds one, the anteater uses its sharp claws to tear inside—and dinner is served!

A Tongue like No Other

The giant anteater also boasts one of the world's weirdest *tongues*. Reaching up to two feet in length, this slurp-tastic structure can extend from its mouth up to 150 times a minute, with as many as 35,000 insects gobbled up daily! Anteaters are also **edentate**, which means they have no teeth! Instead, they use their tongue to smush insects against the roof of their mouths. This helps them better digest their food.

Name: Giant anteater

Species name: *Myrmecophaga tridactyla*

Size: They can reach sizes of 6 to 8 feet (1.8–2.4 meters) in length, from head to tail.

Diet: Almost exclusively ants and termites, and they rarely drink water (instead getting moisture from food or water left on plants after it rains)

Habitat: The wetlands, tropical forests, and grasslands of Central and South America

Predators and threats: They have been **extirpated** from some areas of Central America, with habitat loss being a key threat. Their main wild predators are pumas and jaguars. They are also sometimes hunted or poached by humans.

Big as a RED KANGAROO

12 bananas (height)

Meet the big red roo! Australia is the driest continent in the world, and the sun can be scorching hot. What's a KANGAROO to do? Take a spit bath! By licking and dripping gooey saliva onto their forearms, kangaroos can lower their body temperature. As the saliva evaporates, their skin—and the blood vessels beneath it—cools down, circulating cooler blood throughout the body!

Elasto-Power!

You're probably familiar with the trademark kangaroo hop. But why don't these **macropods** just walk once in a while? The answer is . . . they can't! Kangaroos can't move their back legs independently of each other. But good news for roos—scientists have found that, at high speeds, hopping is one of the most efficient ways for land mammals to travel. This is because their tendons act as springs, harnessing **elastic energy** that's transferred from one jump to the next.

Name: Red kangaroo

Species name: *Macropus rufus*

Size: Males stand up to 6 feet (1.8 meters) tall, with a tail of 3 feet 11 inches (1.2 meters); females are smaller, from 2 feet 9 inches to 3 feet 5 inches tall (84–104 centimeters), with a tail of 2 feet 2 inches to 2 feet 9 inches (66–84 centimeters).

Diet: Grasses, shrubs, and herbs

Habitat: The plains, grasslands, woodlands, open forests, and deserts of central Australia

Predators and threats: These animals are hunted by humans for their hides and meat, and can be struck by cars.

Big as a GREEN ANACONDA

60 bananas (length)

No collection of colossal creatures would be complete without the world's most stupendously sizable snake. The **GREEN ANACONDA** is the world's heaviest snake, weighing in at over five hundred pounds! Unlike many other snakes, anacondas don't lay eggs. Instead, they are **ovoviviparous.** This means that baby anacondas grow inside of eggs, but those eggs hatch inside the mom's body *before* the little snakes slither out into the world. Anacondas can give birth to forty babies at a time!

Rotten Rumors and Reputations

Scared of snakes? You're not alone. **Ophidiophobia,** or the fear of snakes, is one of the most common fears among people. This dread that many humans feel when they spot a snake might even be rooted in **evolution,** to keep us safe from dangerous animals. Anacondas' size and their mysterious lifestyles make for excellent nightmare fuel, and despite being nonvenomous, they are even killed on sight in some areas. But like all misunderstood predators, there's no need to be scared of them . . . unless you're a capybara!

Name: Green anaconda

Species name: *Eunectes murinus*

Size: About 20 to 30 feet long (6.1–9.1 meters) and weighing up to 550 pounds (249 kilograms)

Diet: Capybaras, caimans, jaguars, wild pigs, deer, turtles, tapirs, dogs, sheep, birds, and other snakes

Habitat: Slow-moving streams, swamps, and marshes of the tropical rainforests in the Amazon and Orinoco basins

Predators and threats: They have no natural predators as adults, but they are killed by people who fear them. They are also hunted for their skin and suffer from habitat loss as a result of deforestation.

Big as a KĀKĀPŌ

4 bananas (height)

Not all animal giants are scary—some are downright adorable! The KĀKĀPŌ is the world's heaviest parrot and also happens to be the only species of parrot that can't fly. But who needs flight when you've got excellent hiking, climbing, and jumping abilities? These jumbo parrots also have one more claim to fame: they smell great! Scientists report they have a sugary, musty scent. How *sweet*!

Nighttime Serenades

Want to attend a kākāpō concert? You're in luck! When **breeding season** arrives, male kākāpōs gather together in breeding territories called **leks** to attract female attention. They'll position themselves next to rock faces or hilltops and emit a loud, low-frequency *BOOM* into the night. After 20 to 30 booms, they'll change their call to a sharp *ching* sound. These *booming-chinging* concerts can last up to eight hours a night for the entire breeding season!

BOOM CHING BOOM CHING CHING BOOM!

Name: Kākāpō

Species name: *Strigops habroptilus*

Size: About 23 to 25 inches tall (58–64 centimeters), weighing anywhere from 2 to 9 pounds (0.9–4.1 kilograms)

Diet: Leaves, flowers, buds, fern fronds, bark, **rhizomes**, fruit, and seeds

Habitat: Once widespread throughout New Zealand, kākāpōs are now only found on three small islands (Codfish Island/Whenua Hou, Little Barrier Island/Hauturu, and Anchor Island). They live in forested areas, scrub, herb fields, and grasslands.

Predators and threats: Critically endangered, kākāpōs nearly went extinct due to human hunting and being preyed on by **introduced animals** like cats, ferrets, and stoats. Today, roughly 210 birds exist, and they are monitored closely. Their eggs are vulnerable to rats as well.

Big as a GOLIATH BIRDEATER

2 bananas (length)

Here's one spider you don't want to find in your shoe! Despite its name, the **GOLIATH BIRDEATER** doesn't eat birds *that* often. It prefers to eat **invertebrates**—but will also chow down on toads, rodents, bats, snakes, and small lizards. Unlike some other spiders, these awesome **arachnids** don't spin webs. They prefer to wait for prey to scurry close and then they *POUNCE,* injecting their venom with four-inch fangs.

Living Velcro?

What do goliath birdeaters and Velcro have in common? It's all in the leg hair! Goliath birdeaters have special hairs called **setae** on their first and second pairs of legs. When they're in trouble, they'll rub these legs together and create a hissing sound, similar to the sound of Velcro being pulled apart. These **stridulations** can be heard up to fifteen feet away and tell predators "Stay back or you'll regret it!"

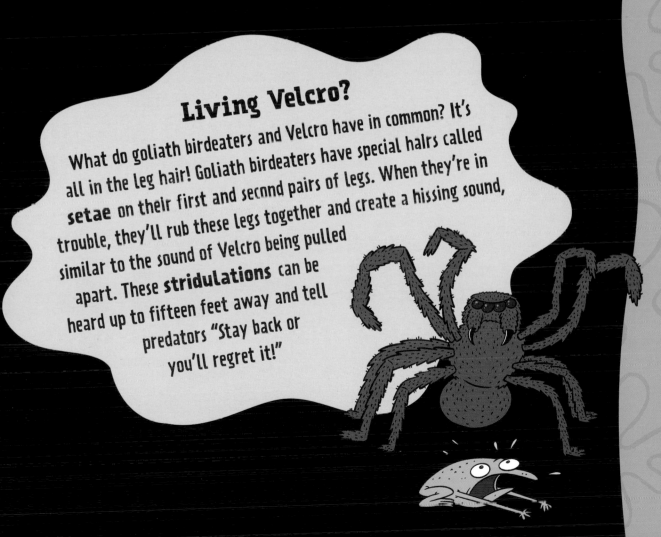

Name: Goliath birdeater

Species name: *Theraphosa blondi*

Size: A legspan of up to 1 foot (30 centimeters)

Diet: Worms, bats, insects, rodents, toads, frogs, lizards, snakes, and (rarely) some birds

Habitat: Goliath birdeaters build deep burrows within rocks and roots, residing in damp rainforests of South America. They are also sometimes kept as pets and bred in captivity.

Predators and threats: Spider wasps, snakes, and tarantulas will all prey on these animals, and some humans will eat them as well, roasted in banana leaves. They are particularly vulnerable when **molting,** as it takes several days for their **exoskeletons** to harden. Habitat destruction is their biggest threat.

The Handy, Dandy Banana Scale!

Every animal in this book is colossal for its kind, but you can use the chart below (and your handy banana scale!) to explore their relative sizes.

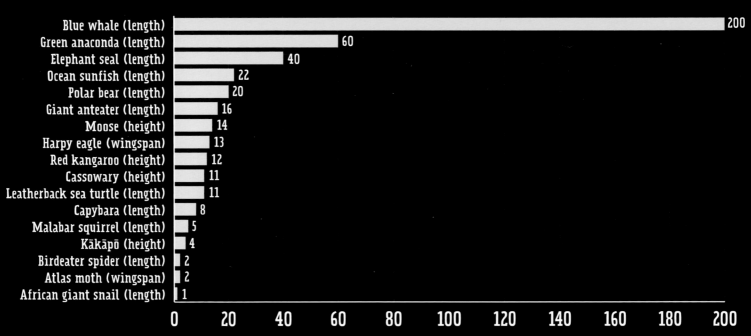

Creature Banana Count!

Animal	Bananas
Blue whale (length)	200
Green anaconda (length)	60
Elephant seal (length)	40
Ocean sunfish (length)	22
Polar bear (length)	20
Giant anteater (length)	16
Moose (height)	14
Harpy eagle (wingspan)	13
Red kangaroo (height)	12
Cassowary (height)	11
Leatherback sea turtle (length)	11
Capybara (length)	8
Malabar squirrel (length)	5
Kākāpō (height)	4
Birdeater spider (length)	2
Atlas moth (wingspan)	2
African giant snail (length)	1

0 20 40 60 80 100 120 140 160 180 200

How many bananas are you?!

You can also use this chart to compare these animals with other objects or people. With a friend or family member, use the banana in the book to measure yourself. Roughly how many bananas tall are you? How does that compare to the measurements in the chart above? Are you as big as a capybara? What about a cassowary?

A blue whale is over two school buses long!

A cassowary can be taller than the average woman in the United States!

An atlas moth is almost the size of a dinner plate!

Say What?! A Glossary of Useful Words

Some of the words in the text are in **bold.** If you didn't understand them, you can use the list below to learn their definition.

- **Amphipods:** small crustaceans, including types of beach fleas and sand hoppers
- **Arachnids:** a group of animals that includes spiders, scorpions, mites, and ticks
- **Arboreal:** living mainly in trees
- **Bioluminescent:** when an animal or organism can make its own light
- **Breeding season:** a period of time when animals mate
- **Calving:** when female animals give birth to a calf (seen in cows, elephants, whales, hippos, and more!)
- **Camouflage:** hiding from predators, often by blending in with the surroundings
- **Canopy:** the upper layer of trees in a forest
- **Carapace:** the bony layer covering the back of a turtle
- **Carnivores:** animals that eat meat
- **Casque:** a piece of hard armor found on the head of cassowaries
- **Cetaceans:** large aquatic animals like whales, dolphins, and porpoises
- **Civets:** slender, cat-like mammals that eat meat
- **Coloration:** the arrangement of colors or shades
- **Copepods:** extremely tiny, shimp-like creatures that are found virtually anywhere with water
- **Coprophagy:** when an animal eats its own poop
- **Deciduous:** relating to trees or shrubs that lose their leaves seasonally
- **Delicacy:** something that is considered a luxury to eat
- **Edentate:** having no teeth
- **Elastic energy:** energy stored, such as in a coiled spring
- **Epipelagic:** relating to the surface part of the ocean, where light can penetrate the water
- **Evolution:** the process by which organisms change over many years and generations

- **Exoskeletons:** the hard body coverings of some invertebrate animals, particularly arthropods
- **Extinction:** when an animal no longer exists in the world
- **Extirpated:** when something is destroyed or wiped out
- **Feral:** relating to a wild animal
- **Foot:** in a snail, the flattened body that is used for locomotion
- **Generalist predators:** animals that are able to survive in varied environments, eating a wide variety of prey
- **Harem:** a group of female animals sharing a single mate
- **Hydrodynamic:** relating to something that can move easily through the water
- **Introduced animals:** animals that are brought to a location that they don't normally belong in
- **Invasive species:** a living thing that is introduced to a new place where it typically causes damage
- **Invertebrates:** animals without backbones, such as arthropods, mollusks, and worms
- **Keratin:** a protein that is found in numerous animals, forming hair, nails, hooves, feathers, and claws
- **Leks:** assembly areas where male animals carry out behaviors to attract mates
- **Low-frequency:** describing slow sound vibrations that create a low note
- **Macropods:** plant-eating marsupials with powerful hind legs and feet, and long, muscular tails
- **Mesopelagic:** relating to a zone of the ocean where only some light can penetrate
- **Migration:** when animals move from one place to another at certain times of the year

- **Mollusk:** one of a group of soft-bodied animals, including snails, slugs, oysters, clams, and octopuses
- **Molting:** when an animal casts off part of its body
- **Ophidiophobia:** fear of snakes
- **Oral papillae:** bumps or spikes found on the top of the tongue
- **Ovoviviparous:** producing eggs that are hatched within the mother's body
- **Parabolic reflector:** a surface that collects and concentrates sound or energy
- **Parasitize:** to take nourishment from another organism, by acting as a parasite
- **Proboscis:** in mammals, a long and mobile nose, similar to a trunk
- **Radiator:** something that lets off heat
- **Radula:** a toothed ribbon inside the mouths of snails and most other mollusks

- **Rhizomes:** the underground stems of a plant
- **Rutting season:** a period of mating and courtship in some animals
- **Semi-aquatic:** when an organism spends some of its life in water
- **Setae:** stiff hairs or bristles
- **Spawning season:** a period of time in which fish and some other animals release eggs and sperm into the water around them
- **Stridulations:** sounds made by rubbing certain body parts together
- **Terrestrial:** living or growing on land
- **Vegetation:** the plants of a particular habitat
- **Ventral pleats:** the grooves on the undersurface of the throats of some whales
- **Vertebrate:** an animal that has a backbone or spinal column, including mammals, birds, reptiles, and fishes
- **Vibrissae:** long, stiff hairs on some mammals' faces, used as organs of touch
- **Voracious:** wanting to eat a large amount of food

THIS IS A BORZOI BOOK PUBLISHED BY ALFRED A. KNOPF   Text copyright © 2021 by Jess Keating   Jacket photograph used under license from Shutterstock.com   Interior illustrations copyright © 2021 by David DeGrand

All rights reserved. Published in the United States by Alfred A. Knopf, an imprint of Random House Children's Books, a division of Penguin Random House LLC, New York.

Knopf, Borzoi Books, and the colophon are registered trademarks of Penguin Random House LLC.

Visit us on the Web! rhcbooks.com   Educators and librarians, for a variety of teaching tools, visit us at RHTeachersLibrarians.com

Library of Congress Cataloging-in-Publication Data is available upon request.

ISBN 978-0-593-30084-8 (trade) — ISBN 978-0-593-30085-5 (lib. bdg.) — ISBN 978-0-593-30086-2 (ebook)

The illustrations in this book were created using ink and digital coloring.

Book design by Sarah Hokanson and Monique Razzouk

MANUFACTURED IN CHINA   November 2021   10 9 8 7 6 5 4 3 2 1   First Edition

Random House Children's Books supports the First Amendment and celebrates the right to read.

PHOTO CREDITS: Ruler photo (pg. 6) © Quang Ho/Shutterstock • Malabar giant squirrel photo (pg. 8) © Sandesh Kadur/naturepl.com • Blue whale photo (pg. 10) © SCIEPRO/Getty Images • African giant snail photo (jacket) © majivecka/Shutterstock • African giant snail photo (pg. 12) © Konrad Wothe/naturepl.com • Moose photo (pg. 14) © S. J. Krasemann/Getty Images • Leatherback sea turtle photo (pg. 16) © Shane P. White/Minden Pictures • Cassowary photo (pg. 18) © Konrad Wothe/naturepl.com • Polar bear photo (pg. 20) © Arturo de Frias Photography/Getty Images • Atlas moth photo (pg. 22) © Dibyendu Sarkar/Getty Images • Capybara photo (pg. 24) © Sean Crane/Minden Pictures • Harpy eagle photo (pg. 26) © Jose A. Nicoli • Elephant seal photo (pg. 28) © Justin Mertens/Getty Images • Ocean sunfish photo (pg. 30) © Barcroft Media/Getty Images • Giant anteater photo (pg. 32) © Stan Osolinski/Getty Images • Red kangaroo photo (pg. 34) © Jami Tarris/Getty Images • Green anaconda photo (pg. 36) © Sylvain Cordier/Getty Images • Kākāpō photo (pg. 38) © Brent Stephenson/naturepl.com • Goliath birdeater photo (pg. 40) © Piotr Naskrecki/Minden Pictures